Your Mission to Venus

by Christine Zuchora-Walske
illustrated by Scott Burroughs

Content Consultant
Diane M. Bollen, Research Scientist,
Cornell University

visit us at www.abdopublishing.com

Published by Magic Wagon, a division of the ABDO Group, 8000 West 78th
Street, Edina, Minnesota, 55439. Copyright © 2012 by Abdo Consulting
Group, Inc. International copyrights reserved in all countries. All rights
reserved. No part of this book may be reproduced in any form without
written permission from the publisher.

Looking Glass Library™ is a trademark and logo of Magic Wagon.

Printed in the United States of America, North Mankato, Minnesota.
052011
092011

 THIS BOOK CONTAINS AT LEAST 10% RECYCLED MATERIALS.

Text by Christine Zuchora-Walske
Illustrations by Scott Burroughs
Edited by Holly Saari
Series design and cover production by Becky Daum
Interior production by Christa Schneider

Library of Congress Cataloging-in-Publication Data
Zuchora-Walske, Christine.
  Your mission to Venus / by Christine Zuchora-Walske ; illustrated by Scott
Burroughs.
     p. cm. — (The planets)
  Includes index.
  ISBN 978-1-61641-684-3
  1. Venus (Planet)—Juvenile literature. 2. Venus (Planet)—Exploration—
Juvenile literature. I. Burroughs, Scott, ill. II. Title.
  QB621.Z83 2012
  523.42—dc22
                                    2011010662

Table of Contents

Imagine You Could Go

Have you ever heard about Earth's "sister"? It's Venus! The two planets are almost the same size, so people have called them siblings.

They're not really sisters, though. You can live on Earth, but you can't live on Venus. The heavy, poisonous atmosphere would crush and choke you. The heat would melt your body. You can't even visit Venus. But imagine if you could . . .

SOLAR SYSTEM

SUN

MERCURY
VENUS
EARTH
MARS
JUPITER
SATURN
URANUS
NEPTUNE

Solar System

To find your way, you carry a map of our solar system. Your map shows eight planets that orbit the sun.

Venus is the second planet from the sun and Earth's nearest neighbor. You can see Venus easily from Earth. Venus is the second-brightest object in our night sky. Only our moon is brighter.

Venus got its name because of its brightness. Ancient Greeks thought Venus was very pretty. They named it after their most beautiful goddess.

Gravity

Before you get there, you read more about Venus. It is just a little bit smaller than Earth. It's only a little less heavy. That means that gravity on Venus is similar to Earth's, too. Gravity is a powerful force in the universe. It pulls things together.

Gravity on Earth is what makes things fall to the ground. It gives things weight. Your arms and legs will feel just a little lighter on Venus than they do on Earth.

SIZE COMPARISON

EARTH

VENUS

SPACE BONES

9

DOMINOES

CHESS

CHECKERS

10

Distance from Earth

An orbit is the path a planet takes on its trip around the sun. The orbits of Venus and Earth are about 26 million miles (41 million km) apart. Even though you are traveling on the world's fastest rocket, it is still going to take more than a month to get to Venus.

Humans have sent many spacecraft to study Venus. None carried passengers. All took three or more months to reach Venus.

Years and Days

Your birthday is coming up! On Earth you're turning ten, but on Venus you're 16. A year is the time a planet takes to orbit the sun once. One year on Earth is 365 days. One year on Venus is only 225 days.

On Earth a day is 24 hours. That is the time it takes for the planet to spin fully around on its axis. On Venus, one day is 5,832 hours. Venus is one of two planets in the solar system that spins clockwise. The other is Uranus. Venus spins slower than all the other planets.

On Earth, the sun rises in the east. On Venus, the sun rises in the west. This is because Venus spins the opposite direction of Earth.

Atmosphere

Your spacecraft draws close to Venus. You peek out the window and see yellow clouds. These clouds are made of acid. The acid eats away at metal and other materials. Luckily, your rocket has a special, protective coating.

You smell something, too. The clouds smell like rotten eggs! Lightning flashes and thunder booms outside your rocket.

The planet's highest clouds race around the planet. Strong winds push them at about 224 miles per hour (360 km/h). That's faster than most tornadoes on Earth.

You keep traveling through the atmosphere. The layer of gases is thick and presses hard on the surface of Venus. You remember reading that the pressure on Venus is 90 times more than Earth's. Standing on Venus might feel a bit like standing on the bottom of Earth's deep oceans.

As your spacecraft gets closer to the surface, the clouds thin. The wind lets up.

Temperature

You land your craft on Venus and look around. Clouds hide the sun. But you can feel the blazing heat. Temperatures can reach about 860 degrees Fahrenheit (460°C). That's hot enough to melt lead, a kind of metal. Venus is the hottest planet in our solar system.

Several spacecraft from Earth have landed on Venus. But the heat destroyed each within three hours.

Surface

You hop in your rover. You drive all over Venus. The ground is rocky and dry. You see sand dunes, or large hills of wind-blown sand. Flat plains cover most of Venus. But Venus has thousands of volcanoes, too.

The core of Venus is made of iron. Scientists think it is part solid and part liquid.

You drive your rover toward the north pole and onto Ishtar Terra. It's one of two plateaus on Venus. It's as big as Australia!

Soon you see Maxwell Montes, the highest mountain on Venus. It's about seven miles (11 km) tall. You climb it and reach the top. On the peak, you are higher up than if you were on top of Earth's Mount Everest.

The other plateau on Venus is called Aphrodite Terra. It's as big as South America.

As you explore Venus, you drive around many large craters. Craters are holes created when space objects crash into a planet. Venus has no small craters. Small objects burn up in the thick, hot atmosphere before they hit the ground.

It has been a long day. You've seen some amazing sights! But there is still so much to learn about Venus. After sleeping, you'll explore more questions scientists are trying to answer. Have there ever been oceans on Venus? Has there ever been microscopic life on the planet? You will soon find out!

DOMINOES

CHESS

CHECKERS

How Do Scientists Know about Venus?

People have been watching Venus for thousands of years. The telescope was invented in the early 1600s. Italian scientist Galileo Galilei was the first to turn one toward the sky. He studied Venus and other planets with a telescope in 1610.

For the next few centuries, scientists continued to study Venus through telescopes. In the 1950s and 1960s, they began using radar to observe Venus. This helped scientists measure the temperature on Venus and discover the speed it spins at.

The first spacecraft humans successfully sent to study another planet was *Mariner 2*. It flew by Venus in December 1962. It carried no astronauts. It measured temperatures on the surface and studied the atmosphere.

In the early 1990s, the *Magellan* spacecraft used radar to map the surface of Venus. In 2005, scientists sent a spacecraft called *Venus Express* to orbit the planet and study the atmosphere and weather patterns.

Venus Facts

Position: Second planet from sun

Distance from sun: 67 million miles (108 million km)

Diameter (distance through the planet's middle): 7,521 miles (12,104 km)

Length of orbit (year): 225 Earth days

Length of rotation (day): 5,832 hours

Gravity: About nine-tenths as strong as Earth's gravity

Number of moons: 0

Words to Know

atmosphere—the layer of gases surrounding a planet.

core—the center of a planet.

crater—a dip in the ground shaped like a large bowl.

gas—a substance that spreads out to fit what it is in, like air in a tire.

gravity—the force that pulls a smaller object toward a larger object.

orbit—to travel around something, usually in an oval path.

plateau—an area of flat, high land.

solar system—a star and the objects, such as planets, that travel around it.

tornado—a violent, spinning column of air shaped like a funnel.

volcano—a mountain from which hot liquid rock or steam comes out.

Learn More

Books

Jefferis, David. *Hot Planets*. New York: Crabtree, 2008.

Landau, Elaine. *Venus*. New York: Children's Press, 2008.

Yasuda, Anita. *Explore the Solar System!* White River Junction, VT: Nomad Press, 2009.

Web Sites

To learn more about Venus, visit ABDO Group online at **www.abdopublishing.com**. Web sites about Venus are featured on our Book Links page. These links are routinely monitored and updated to provide the most current information available.

Index